The King's Ears

by Helen Docherty
Illustrated by Elena Iarussi

Shakespeare Infant School
Eastleigh, Hampshire
SO50 4FZ
Tel: 023 0573888

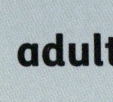

Long ago, there was a king who ruled over a vast land. King March was kind and good, and everybody loved him ... but he was not happy.

The king had a terrible secret, and he didn't want anybody to know. He had the ears of a horse!

adult

King March usually kept his ears hidden under his long hair and his crown.

However, one day, the queen said, "It's my birthday tomorrow. You need a haircut!"

She called for Bevan, the barber, to cut the king's hair. "Be quick," she said, as she left the room.

<u>Within</u> a few minutes, the king's hair lay on the floor. Bevan could see the king's ears!

"You must promise to keep this a secret <u>between</u> us," said the king.

Bevan had to cut the king's hair very quickly. Do you ever have to do something quickly, <u>within</u> a short amount of time?

adult

Bevan tried very hard not to say anything, but it made him unhappy. He hated keeping secrets. He knew that he would not be <u>able</u> to keep the king's secret for very long.

Later that day, Bevan went to the river. He decided to whisper the king's secret.

Do you think you would be <u>able</u> to keep the king's secret? Why/why not?

child

Bevan bent down to tell the reeds.

adult

Meanwhile ...

King March was planning a party for the queen's birthday. He had sent for the best piper in the land.

On her way to the party, the piper passed the river. The reed in her pipe was beginning to get old and thin.

The reed in the pipe was beginning to get old. Do you have any toys that are beginning to get old? How can you tell?

adult

It was the evening of the party. Everybody was excited to be there.

"Play us a tune!" King March called to the piper.

The piper blew into her pipe with its new reed from the river. However, instead of playing music, the pipe began to sing: *"The king has the ears of a horse!"*

There was a terrible silence.

adult

"Play again," ordered the king. "Properly, this time!"

The piper thought she would <u>rather</u> be anywhere else in the world at that moment. However, she had to obey the king.

Once again, the pipe sang: *"The king has the ears of a horse!"*

The king glared at the piper and at Bevan. He felt they were both to blame.

Why do you think that the piper would <u>rather</u> be somewhere else? Have you ever had to go somewhere when you'd <u>rather</u> be somewhere else?

adult

Then, King March <u>realized</u> that it was too late. His secret was out.

"Who cares what your ears look like?" said the queen.

The king was thoughtful for a moment, then said, "You are right! Who cares?"

He lifted his crown off his head.

What has the king <u>realized</u>? What would you do if you were the king?

Read the words

down

spoil

ear

fair

sure

thicker